THE FINDING OF
THE "MAYFLOWER"

By

RENDEL HARRIS

WITH THE ESSAY
The Myth of the "Mayflower"
BY G. K. CHESTERTON

First published in 1920

Read & Co.

Copyright © 2020 Read & Co. History

This edition is published by Read & Co. History,
an imprint of Read & Co.

This book is copyright and may not be reproduced or copied in any
way without the express permission of the publisher in writing.

British Library Cataloguing-in-Publication Data
A catalogue record for this book is available
from the British Library.

Read & Co. is part of Read Books Ltd.
For more information visit
www.readandcobooks.co.uk

CONTENTS

ILLUSTRATIONS

THE MAYFLOWER

An Excerpt from
The Encyclopedia Americana, 1920

The name of the vessel in which the Pilgrim Fathers, or first colonists in New England, sailed to this country in 1620. The *Mayflower* was a vessel of 180 tons. She set sail from Southampton, England, on 5 Aug. 1620, in company with her sister ship, the *Speedwell*, but the courage of the captain and the crew of the latter vessel failing, both ships put back to port. Finally on 6/17 September the *Mayflower* again spread her sails from Plymouth, having on board as passengers 41 men and their families, 102 persons in all. They succeeded in crossing the Atlantic after a stormy voyage of 63 days. They intended to go to the mouth of the Hudson River but the captain of the *Mayflower* took them to Cape Cod.

They landed at Plymouth, Mass., at a point where Plymouth Rock, a huge granite boulder, stands at the water's edge.

The following is a copy of the covenant agreed upon by these first settlers of Massachusetts, signed and subscribed on board the Mayflower at Cape Cod, 10/21 Nov. 1620, two days after the ship came to anchor.

THE MAYFLOWER COMPACT

In the name of God Amen!

We whose names are underwritten, the loyal subjects of our dread sovereign Lord, King James, by the grace of God, of Great Britain, France and Ireland, King, Defender of the Faith, etc., have undertaken for the glory of God and the advancement of the Christian faith, and honor of our King and Country, a voyage to plant the first colony in the northern parts of Virginia; do by these presents, solemnly and mutually, in the presence of God and of one another covenant and combine ourselves together into a civil body politic for our better ordering and preservation, and furthermore of the ends aforesaid; and by virtue hereof to enact, constitute and frame just and equal laws, ordinances, acts, constitutions, and offices from time to time, as shall be thought most mete and convenient for the general good of the colony; unto which we promise all due submission and obedience.

In witness whereof we have hereunto subscribed our names, at Cape Cod, the 11th of November, in the year of the reign of our sovereign Lord, King James of England, France and Ireland, the Eighteenth, and of Scotland the Fifty-fourth, Anno Domini 1620.

THE MYTH
OF THE "MAYFLOWER"

By G. K. Chesterton

Agnosticism, the ancient confession of ignorance, was a singularly sane and healthy thing so far as it went. Unfortunately it has not gone as far as the twentieth century. It has declared in all ages, as a heathen chief declared in the dark ages, that the life of a man is like the flight of a bird across a firelit room, because we know nothing of whence it comes or whither it goes. It would seem natural to apply it not only to man but to mankind. But the moderns do not apply the same principle but the very opposite principle. They specialize in the unknown origins and in the unknown future. They dwell on the prehistoric and on the post-historic or prophetic; and neglect only the historic. They will give a most detailed description of the habits of the bird when he was a sort of pterodactyl only faintly to be traced in a fossil. They will give an equally detailed description of the habits of the bird a hundred years hence, when he shall have turned into a super-bird, or the dove of universal peace. But the bird in the hand is worth far less to them than the two mysterious birds in these two impenetrable bushes. Thus they will publish a portrait with life, letters, and tabletalk of the Missing Link, although he is missing; they will publish a plan and documented history of how the Social Revolution happened, though it has not happened yet. It is the men who are not missing and the revolutions that have happened that they have rather a habit of overlooking. Anyone who has argued, for instance, with the young Jewish intellectuals who are the brain of Bolshevism knows that their whole system turns on the two pivots of the prehistoric and the prophetic. They talk of the Communism of prehistoric ages as if it were a thing like the Crusades in the Middle Ages; not even a probable conjecture but a proved and familiar fact. They will tell you exactly how private property arose in primitive times, just as if they had been there. And then they will take one gigantic leap over all human history, and tell you about the inevitable Communism of the future. Nothing seems to matter unless it is either new enough to be foretold or old enough to be forgotten.

Mr. H. G. Wells has hit off his human habit in the account of a very human character, the American girl who glorifies Stonehenge in his last novel. I do not make Mr. Wells responsible for her opinions, though she is an attractive person and much too good for her Lothario. But she interests me here because she typifies very truly another variation upon this same tendency. To the prehistoric and the post-historic must be added a third thing, which may be called the unhistoric. I mean the bad teaching of real history that such intelligent people so often suffer. She sums up exactly what I mean when she says humorously that Stonehenge has been "kept from her," that Notre Dame is far less important, and that this is the real starting-point of the "Mayflower." Now the "Mayflower" is a myth. It is an intensely interesting example of a real modern myth. I do not mean of course that the "Mayflower" never sailed, any more than I admit that King Arthur never lived or that Roland never died. I do not mean that the incident had no historic interest, or that the men who figured in it had no heroic qualities; any more than I deny that Charlemagne was a great man because the legend says he was two hundred years old; any more than I deny that the resistance of Roman Britain to the heathen invasion was valiant and valuable, because the legend says that Arthur at Mount Badon killed nine hundred men with his own hand. I mean that there exists in millions of modern minds a traditional image or vision called the "Mayflower," which has far less relation to the real facts than Charlemagne's two hundred years or Arthur's nine hundred corpses. Multitudes of people in England and America, as intelligent and sympathetic as the young lady in Mr. Wells' novel, think of the "Mayflower" as an origin or archetype like the Ark or at least the Argo. Perhaps it would be an exaggeration to say that they think the "Mayflower" discovered America. They do really talk as if the "Mayflower" populated America. Above all, they talk as if the establishment of New England had been the first and formative example of the expansion of England. They believe that English expansion was a Puritan experiment; and that an expansion of Puritan ideas was also the expansion of what have been claimed as English ideas, especially ideas of liberty. The Puritans of New England were champions of religious freedom, seeking to found a newer and freer state beyond the sea, and thus becoming the origin and model of modern democracy. All this betrays a lack of exactitude. It is certainly nearer to exact truth to say that Merlin built the castle at Camelot by magic, or that Roland broke the mountains in pieces with his unbroken sword. For at least the old fables are faults on the right side. They are symbols of the truth and not of the opposite of the truth. They described Roland as brandishing his unbroken sword against the Moslems, but not in favour of the Moslems. And the New England Puritans would have regarded the establishment of real religious liberty exactly as Roland would have regarded the establishment of the religion of Mahound. The fables described Merlin as building a palace for a king and not a public hall for the London School of Economics. And it would be quite as sensible to read the Fabian politics of Mr. Sidney Webb into the local kingships of the Dark Ages, as to read anything remotely resembling modern liberality into the most savage of all the savage theological frenzies of the seventeenth century. Thus the "Mayflower" is not merely a fable, but is much more false than fables generally are. The revolt of the Puritans against the Stuarts was really a revolt *against* religious toleration. I do not say the Puritans were never persecuted by their opponents; but I do say, to their great honour and glory, that the Puritans never descended to the hypocrisy of pretending for a moment that they did not mean to persecute their opponents. And in the main their quarrel with the Stuarts was that the Stuarts would not persecute those opponents enough. Not only was it then the Catholics who were proposing toleration, but it was they who had already actually established toleration in the State of Maryland, before the Puritans began to establish the most intolerant sort of intolerance in the State of New England. And if the fable is fabulous touching the emancipation of religion, it is yet more fabulous touching the expansion of empire. That had been started long before either New England or Maryland, by Raleigh who started it in Virginia. Virginia is still perhaps the most English of the states, certainly more English than New England. And it was also the most typical and important of the states, almost up to Lee's last battle in the Wilderness. But I have only taken the "Mayflower" as an example of the general truth; and in a way the truth has its consoling side. Modern men are not allowed to have any history; but at least nothing can prevent men from having legends. We have thus before us, in a very true and typical modern picture, the two essential parts of modern culture. It consists first of false history and second of fancy history. What the American tourist believed about Plymouth Rock was untrue; what she believed about Stonehenge was only unfounded. The popular story of Primitive Man cannot be proved. The popular story of Puritanism can be disproved. I can fully sympathize with Mr. Wells and his heroine in feeling the imaginative stimulus of mysteries like Stonehenge; but the imagination springs from the mystery; that is, the imagination springs from the ignorance. It is the very greatness of Stonehenge that there is very little of it left. It is its chief feature to be featureless. We are very naturally and rightly moved to mystical emotions about signals from so far away along the path of the past; but part of the poetry lies in our inability really to read the signals. And this is what gives an interest, and even an irony, to the comparison half consciously invoked by the American lady herself when she asked "What's Notre Dame to this?" And the answer that should be given to her is: "Notre Dame, compared to this, is *true*. It is history. It is humanity. It is what has really happened, what we know has really happened, what we know is really happening still. It is the central fact of your own civilization. And it is the thing that has really been kept from you."

Notre Dame is not a myth. Notre Dame is not a theory. Its interest does not spring from ignorance but from knowledge; from a culture complicated with a hundred controversies and revolutions. It is not featureless, but carved into an incredible forest and labyrinth of fascinating features, any one of which we could talk about for days. It is not great because there is little of it, but great because there is a great deal of it. It is true that though there is a great deal of it, Puritans may not be allowed to see a great deal in it; whether they were those brought over in the "Mayflower" or only those brought up on the "Mayflower." But that is not the fault of Notre Dame; but of the extraordinary evasion by which such people can dodge to right and left of it, taking refuge in things more recent or things more remote. Notre Dame, on its merely human side, is mediæval civilization, and therefore not a fable or a guess but a great solid determining part of modern civilization.

It is the whole modern debate about the guilds; for such cathedrals were built by the guilds. It is the whole modern question of religion and irreligion; for we know what religion it stands for, while we really have not a notion what religion Stonehenge stands for. A Druid temple is a ruin, and a Puritan ship by this time may well be called a wreck. But a church is a challenge; and that is why it is not answered.

A CHAPTER FROM
Fancies Versus Fads, 1923

INTRODUCTION

In the present volume the reader will find what, I suppose, may be described as the culmination and crown of my researches into the story of the Pilgrim Fathers. The discovery here recorded will, without doubt, send a thrill of genuine emotion and interest through the English-speaking and the liberty-loving world. The variation in the terms is necessary, for we cannot too often remind ourselves that in the training of the Pilgrims, Holland occupies as important a place as England, and, in some respects, a more honourable position; for it is Holland who educated the Venturers by freedom, where England educated by persecution; nor must we forget that the eleven years of sanctuary in the beautiful city of Leyden were made possible by the courteous refusal of the Leyden authorities to alienate the Pilgrims at the request of King James and his ambassador, a noble resolve on their part to share their own hardly-won liberties with those who had not yet reached the haven of Freedom, although, as the English officials reported, the Dutch would rather pluck out their eyes than displease His Majesty. So the discovery, which we are now going to describe, will be welcomed as warmly in Holland as in England or the United States, and we shall tell the story in the simplest possible manner.

THE FINDING OF THE "MAYFLOWER".

CHAPTER I.

THE CAMPO SANTO OF THE SOCIETY OF FRIENDS AT JORDANS.

IN the county of Buckingham there is a tract of land which is becoming popularly known as the Milton-and-Penn-country. It is Milton's area of remembrance, chiefly because the village of Chalfont St. Giles contains a cottage where Milton for a short time resided; here he had constant visits from Thomas Ellwood, the Quaker, who had taken the house for him, and describes it as a pretty box in Giles Chalfont, for, as is well known, the Friends have de-sainted the Calendar,[1] just as they discount and disown the titles of nobility supplied by the State. When I knew Giles Chalfont first, the cottage was the residence of the village policeman, whose symbol of authority was on the house in the form of an attached plate; it has since become national property. Here, then, Ellwood found a retreat for Milton in the time of the Great Plague; here he took Latin lessons from the Great Bard and learnt the Italian pronunciation of the language; here the poet gave him the manuscript of *Paradise Lost*, and received when the book was returned, the penetrating question, " Thou hast said much here of *Paradise Lost*, but what hast thou to say of *Paradise Found?*" Ellwood says definitely that this

---

[1] The Church Registers of the time often do the same.

question put the poet in a muse and was the cause of
the production of what Milton strangely believed to be
his greatest work (for poets are the worst judges of the
relative stature of their offspring ; did not Wordsworth
affirm that Laodameia would rank with Lycidas?);
for Ellwood says that, at a later date, when visiting
Milton in London, "he showed me his second poem,
called *Paradise Regained,* and in a pleasant tone, said
to me, ' This is owing to you ; for you put it into my
head, by the question you put to me at Chalfont, which
before I had not thought of'". It cannot be doubted
that Ellwood's question was prompted, not by any de-
sire for the production of another poem, but by the
spiritual views of the Quakers who, with their leader,
George Fox, believed that it was possible to come up
into the Paradise of God, where the whole creation gets
a new smell, beyond what words can utter! He was
putting his finger gently, lovingly, on the elder man's
pulse and recording its beatings, perhaps without a
suspicion on Milton's part as to the inwardness of the
enquiry : "Art thou re-Paradised?" Ellwood was saying.

   This, then, is Milton's country ; but the appearance
of Ellwood on the scene, as house-provider, as guide,
as spiritual philosopher and friend, shows that we are
in Quaker land also : and for this reason it is called
by tourists the Penn country. It might equally have
been called the Ellwood country, or the Penington
country, but the world knows nothing, or next to nothing, of Thomas Ellwood, or of Isaac Penington the
Quaker mystic ; it knows the courtier, and statesman,
and empire-builder ; so let us call it Penn's country :
and then let us note that in this very parish of Giles
Chalfont, is the old Quaker Meeting-House where these

The Old Quaker Meeting-House at Jordans

[To face p. 2

persons of inconsiderable quality[1] worshipped and for worshipping in which they suffered bonds and imprisonment. In front of the Meeting-House is their open-air Westminster Abbey, where they and theirs lie side by side, within ear-shot, as it were, of the truths that Friends have still to tell. No more lovely resting-place for great labourers or great lovers in the whole countryside, or on this side of Paradise itself! It is not surprising that a steady stream of pilgrims come every year into this gracious retreat, to absorb the stillness, and to study the democracy of death in the tiny gravestones, all equal and all alike, and all destitute of such human praises, as are symbolised on monuments by a flying Fame, with rushing wings, and a sound-filled trumpet. Originally the " Hic Jacet " formula was even simpler ; in the first instance, there were no memorial stones at all (though this is not quite certain) ; and it is only in comparatively recent times that an imperfect, uncertain, incomplete attempt has been made, to say that this is William Penn's grave and this Gulielma Penn's, and so on. Many graves (most of them in fact) are still anonymous. As we have said, some of them are doubtfully identified, and in this also there lies an advantage : for when the Mayor of Philadelphia came over to beg the bones of the founder of their city for a shrine in the new City Hall, the Friends were able, not only to reply with the general statement that they do not alienate their sanctities, but also to point out discreetly that it was not possible to say positively which was William Penn's grave and which his first wife's ; clearly it would never have done to embark Gulielma Penn's bones in place of his, and enshrine

---

[1] So described in the Episcopal returns.

them deceitfully in silver that was not their proper resting-place. Mayor Harrison could see that there was no reply to that objection, unless he should volunteer to dig up the whole of the Campo Santo, and replace it in Fairmount Park.

He seemed never to have known the lines in which Freedom spoke by the mouth of Oliver Wendell Holmes :—

> An island is a world, she said,
>   When glory with its dust is blended ;
> And Britain keeps her noble dead
>   Till earth and seas and skies are rended.

Keeps and will keep.

Well! here is the picture of the graveyard ; it is our starting point in our investigation, and may very well be the concluding point of our first chapter.

CHAPTER II.

The Trail Found.

In our previous chapter we made a rapid reference to the Friends' Meeting-House, and the attached graveyard at Jordans, in the county of Bucks. The visitor, who leaves the Great Central Railway, in search of the spot, will find the sign posts advertising him that this is the way to Old Jordans : but in Ellwood's time it was known as New Jordans, and is so described in the account of his funeral. When I was first acquainted with Jordans, it was seldom visited ; the chief event was an annual pilgrimage in the month of May on the part of the Friends attending their yearly meeting in London. (Charles Lamb will tell us what that was like) ; they used to come out here to "smell the air" as

THE OLD QUAKER GRAVEYARD AT JORDANS

[To face p. 4

the Arabs say, and verily it "smells wooingly here," especially after London air and London meetings ; they came, too, to smell the past, which is again a sweet savour of God in Christ to the wise among them, and to those who know that what has been may be.

The annual pilgrimage has, however, fallen into insignificance, not from lack of interest, but from the very opposite. Quakerism in London has annexed this centre, for purposes of colonisation, of education and of religious revival. There is now many times more than a single annual pilgrimage to Mecca. With wise foresight they have purchased, or, to be exact, have repurchased the adjoining farm, in whose kitchen in the seventeenth century Friends used to meet, before the present Meeting-House was built in the year of grace, (for free men and free thought), 1688 : with the farm came to them the farm buildings, of which the most notable was a magnificent old barn, itself of the seventeenth century, and a bit of an old-world sunken garden, such as might at one time have produced the flowers which Perdita remembered to have been dropt by Proserpina from Dis' waggon, or the sweet herbs and simples with which our ancestors used to dispel all the ills that flesh is heir to, and never trouble the doctor about them except in such extreme cases as might almost make a doctor superfluous. These old buildings were appropriated by the Friends for the purpose of propaganda work, for summer-schools, conferences, week-end schools, and the like, in which they have been, in this country, the pioneers, and are still the experts. I had the honour of opening the Old Farm as a Hostel of residence on July the 13th, 1912, when the turning key in the temporarily closed lock served to intimate that fresh opportunities were at hand, "according," to use

5

the Quaker language, " as He that hath the key doth open ".

One of the subordinate duties, in connection with the re-appropriation of the ancient Quaker farm, was the designation of a part of one of the fields as an extension of the original graveyard.[1] It is, as nearly as possible, like to the simplicity of the old; already a row of tiny headstones tell the names and dates of those who lie beneath. There is the grave of Silvanus Thompson, the well-known physicist; a literary man, too, of wide range and real eminence. He had both qualities for writing the Kelvin memoirs; but the grave-stone will not tell you that; it is not the place to record talents that are being judged elsewhere : you will need a cicerone, like myself. And here is the grave of our beloved John St. George Heath, equally simple and equally great. He was caught away from us too soon, in the midst of social problems and dreams of the world's betterment; one that came among us by a deep convincement ; he was my colleague at Woodbrooke for several years, and after that was warden of Toynbee Hall. It was on the day of his funeral, as we stood round the grave for our last farewells in the light of a wintry day, when the very solstice was against us, and the spring equinox had not re-invoked benediction upon the earth, that some one said to me, pointing to the adjacent barn,

---

[1] This had already been enlarged on the 23rd of 6th month 1763 by the purchase of a strip of ground twenty-two yards by ten, by one Samuel Vanderwell, a Dutch convert, who wanted a special sepulture for himself and family. The piece of ground was taken from the Garden Orchard and added to the Friends' Burial Ground (Summers, *Jordans and the Chalfonts*, p. 256).

"THAT BARN IS BUILT OUT OF THE WOOD OF THE 'MAYFLOWER'."

I was busied with thoughts elsewhere, and paid no immediate attention to what was said. Later on the observation came back to me : I found my fingers closing on a clue. Let us see where the local tradition that we had come across is likely to lead us, or if it will lead us anywhere.

CHAPTER III.

THE TRAIL FOLLOWED.

WHEN one began to look round to see whether any one else was saying, or had said, "Mayflower," it was very difficult to pick up the reminiscence. The difficulty was intensified by the intervention of a mocking spirit, that said "which Mayflower?" for, as every one knows who has engaged in a similar investigation, there be many "Mayflowers," some great and some little, in every port of the kingdom, and sometimes more than one in a single port. If anyone doubts this assertion, let him go to the Record Office, and ask to see the Port Books of the City of London, or of any other British haven, and he will soon know what I mean. If one tries to solve the problem as to what became of the "Mayflower" by an appeal to history and to the documents on which history is based, it will not be found a summer's day task : as an expert once remarked in the Record Office, "the man who says he can come here and make a discovery in a few hours is a liar". The search follows two lines of quest : first, an enquiry by the aid of historical method, apart altogether from the clue which I picked up in the graveyard : second, the interrogation of the story of the farm and of the farm buildings, and of the old barn itself, if we can make it break its long silence and open its mouth in evidence. The first method is that which I have adopted in the little book called *The Last of the Mayflower.*[1] The main points to be kept in mind which result from the investigation in this book are as follows:—

The captain and part-owner of the Pilgrim ship which sailed for Virginia[2] in 1620, and which made land in New England, was one Christopher Jones, of Harwich, who brought her from the Greenland whale-fishery into the Thames, and there hired her to the Adventurers who had themselves hired (and almost enslaved) the Pilgrims to their own capitalistic advantage.

Christopher Jones died in 1622, and in 1624 the ship was appraised by the Admiralty for the owners at a very moderate figure, about one-fourth of her natural value ; and this leads Mr. R. G. Marsden to suggest that it was ship-breaker's price, and that she was accordingly broken up, either on the Thames or on the Orwell,[3] and the proceeds divided among the four owners, of whom Christopher Jones' widow counts for one. We,

[1] Published by the Manchester University Press, and by Longmans & Co.

[2] And under a patent from the London Company of Virginia, and not from the Plymouth Company of Virginia, a momentous difference, upon which hung the very future of the United States. Among the *Papers of the Duke of Manchester* described in the *Hist. MSS. Comm., Appendix to 8th Report*, p. 37*b*, is a "note of the shipping and provisions sent and provided for Virginia by the Earl of Southampton and the Company this year 1620"; the list of ships despatched between August, 1620, and February, 1620-21, includes the "Mayflower". The Company regarded her as one of their own ventures.

[3] We shall see later that it was certainly the Thames.

on the contrary, suggested that it was a valuation, not for sale, but for the widow's fourth. On Mr. Marsden's side it may be urged that almost immediately after the Admiralty valuation, two of the owners, named Moore and Child, proceeded to build a new "Mayflower" at Aldeburgh, of the same tonnage, or nearly so, as the original ship and not very far from the headquarters of the ancient vessel. This makes it certain that they had either broken the old one up or sold her into other hands. Our suggestion was that she was sold to Mr. Thomas Horth of Yarmouth, and that she went to the Greenland whale-fishery as before. If this be the right solution, we can trace the ship onward, almost without a break, till 1641. In 1629 and 1630 she carried Puritans and Pilgrims across to New England, and we found the reason for this to lie in the fact that the Greenland Company had in that year forbidden her sailing, as an interference with their monopoly.[1]

The next time we catch sight of the ship, if it be really the same ship, she is carrying goods to New England for John Eliot, the Apostle to the Indians. This is in 1653, and we have shown that she came off from the Greenland fishery and was now owned by an old whale-fisher named Thomas Webber : and we have

[1] She was accompanied on her voyage to New England in 1629 by a sister ship named the "Whale," which again suggested Greenland. I have since found the proof of this : for among the ships that with the "Mayflower" of Yarmouth took out letters of marque in 1626 we find that Nathaniel Wright and others are entered as owning the "Whale of London" of 200 tons burden and with John Ayres as master. Nathaniel Wright is the colleague of Thomas Horth, of Yarmouth, the owner of the "Mayflower," in the Greenland whale-fishery (S. P. Dom., vol. cxv., p. 45). The "Mayflower" and "Whale" are a pair of partners in whaling and in carrying Puritans and Pilgrims to New England.

conjectured that she was broken up soon after this, probably in the Thames.

Thus there are three possibilities before us. First, there is Mr. Marsden's solution, that she was probably broken up in 1624. (He leaves it open, whether she may have passed into other hands.) Next, there is the possibility that she was broken up soon after 1641, when we lose sight of her in the Greenland fishery. Third, she may have come to her end in or about 1655, in which case she would have been broken up in the Thames, where timber is costly [1] and not at Boston or Salem, where it is very cheap. Which of these is the right solution?

Mr. Marsden has the support of Captain John Smith, of Virginian fame, who pours much scorn on the Pilgrims, because they did not ask his advice, nor take him as their leader, but chose to go across the Atlantic in a leaky ship, and so deserved all the sufferings that came upon them. Against this we have the testimony of the crew who "knew she was sound below the water-line," and the fact that she made almost a record passage homeward, going from land to land in a calendar month.

The following sentences in my book express the final conclusion to which I came :—

"It is very doubtful if there is anything more to be said as to the fate of the *Mayflower.* We traced her

---

[1] For the timber famine in this century, due in part to the development of the British Navy, there are significant references in the documentary history of the time. A Proclamation, to which we refer later, of 7 November, 1622, dealing with the manufacture of bricks, begins by saying that timber is scarce and wanted for the Navy. On 29 June, 1641, an Act of Parliament was drafted for regulating the brick industry : it declares that by reason of the scarcity of timber, there is the more use of bricks for building.

[*To face p.* 11

THE OLD BARN AT JORDANS

to Boston and to the year 1654; one is tempted to conjecture that she died (in a nautical sense) not long after. Most likely she was broken up in Boston or perhaps in the Thames on her last voyage to London. Neither in the one case nor the other would there have been any zeal for the apotheosis of her fragments."

The verdict should be qualified by the omission of Boston as the shipbreaker's yard, for reasons given above.

In the course of the investigation we were careful to point out the strength of Mr. Marsden's case. Is there any way of deciding between A.D. 1624, A.D. 1641, and A.D. 1655? We close this chapter with that question.

CHAPTER IV.

THE "MAYFLOWER" FOUND.

Now let us return from the historical investigation to the archæological. Let us examine the old barn at Jordans and see whether the tradition that attaches to it can be verified.

The barn itself is a wooden structure, raised upon a brick base; it is ninety feet long and about twenty feet wide. It has a rough corner-stone at the S.W. angle, which may possibly tell the secret : but there is no inscription over any of the four doors of the barn. The Northern half of the building is raised somewhat above the rest of the barn, probably on account of the inequality in the surface of the ground and to avoid the necessity of digging for level. If one chooses to say that we have two barns joined together, one slightly higher than the other, the description need not be challenged.

When we examine the structure more carefully, we see that it has undergone some repairs and some modern additions. Modern windows have been let in at the N. and S. ends respectively as well as on the E. side. The floor is a modern piece of woodwork, with no possible claim to antiquity. Here is a view, lengthwise, of the whole building. It shows clearly the way in which the structure has been put together.

Now let us make an experiment, and try to see the barn upside down. To avoid the necessity of standing on our heads, or rotating ourselves through two right angles, we will turn our photograph upside down. The result is almost startling ; the appearance of the fabric is precisely like a ship in process of construction ; it is half-grown ; a little more in the way of sheathing and it will be ready to be launched.

Now let us look at the individual timbers to see if they are new products of the British oak, or if they have been already used in some previous structure. If it is ship's timber we shall find the places where the bolts have been inserted. Almost at once we verify that the building is riddled with trenails or with the places that the oaken trenails originally occupied ; and these have no possible relation to the present building. The next thing we notice is that many of the beams have mortise holes, where beam has been let into beam, and these have no connection with the existing building.

Continuing our examination, we find a piece of a beam which was evidently a part of the keel or stem of the ship ; for it has part of the iron keel-plate still attached to it by an iron pin. All the rest of the building shows traces of oaken pins or trenails, as stated above. This is a very remarkable discovery. It is not a case of one barn or building having been used to build another.

[*To face p.* 12

A Part of the Keel or Stem-band

The next thing which we test for is the presence of curved timbers, such as are proper for the knees of a wooden ship; and for which the oak supplies special material. The number of such curved beams is extraordinary. Those split beams which were used in the roof of our barn were so definitely curved that they could not furnish a flat surface for the tiling, and their hollows have had to be filled out with strips of planking, before the roof could be laid on, an observation due to my friend, W. R. Bowron, who made the first examination of the building for me.

The beams are thoroughly impregnated with salt (some of them if not all), as experiment shows. Everything, therefore, points to the conclusion that the old barn was built out of the beams of a dismantled ship; and to that extent the current tradition is abundantly verified.

But was it a "Mayflower," and if so, was it our "Mayflower," or one of the three possible "Mayflowers" to which we alluded in the previous chapter? Here is one test which we can apply.

If we turn to Bradford's *Journal*, we shall find him, in his all-too-brief description of the voyage, noting that "they were incountred many times with crosse winds, and met with many feirce stormes, with which the ship was so shroudly shaken, and her upper works made very leakie, and *one of the maine beames in ye midd ships was bow'd and craked*, which put them in some fear that ye shipe could not be able to perform her vioage. . . . The m(aste)r and others affirmed they knew ye ship to be stronge and firme under water,[1] and for the buckling [2]

[1] There is no reference to the pumps, as would be the case if the ship were really leaking. Capt. John Smith was not speaking nautically when he called the "Mayflower" a leaky ship.

[2] Arber takes this to mean fastening *with a loop of iron*. Azel

13

of the maine beame, there was [said they] a great iron
scrue yᵉ passengers brought out of Holland, which would
raise the beame into his place, yᵉ which being done, the
carpenter and m(aste)r affirmed that with a post put
under it, set firme in the lower deck, and otherways
bound he would make it sufficiente. And as for the
decks and upper works, they would calke them as well
as they could, etc."

Now let us examine the main-beam of our barn. A
glance will show that it has been badly cracked, either
by the contraction which often occurs in timber, or by a
definite accident. Looking more closely we see that
the rupture has been repaired by means of an iron clamp
held in position by a couple of iron screws.[1] Moreover
this was apparently done before the barn was built, as it
is covered in part by the main supporting joist.[2] *The
question therefore arises whether this piece of cracked
timber is the cracked beam of the original "Mayflower".*
Was the clamp remedial or was it preventive?

It may be objected that this clamp is not exactly the
great iron screw which the passengers had brought with
them. Certainly the screw itself, of which Bradford

Ames is very severe on this explanation. "To those familiar with
this old English word it is apparent that when Bradford used it he
intended to do so as the equivalent of *bowing* or *bending*, etc." He
affirms positively that lexicography is against Arber, from which it is
clear that he cannot have been acquainted with the *Oxford Diction-
ary*, which shows that both uses of the word are good Elizabethan
English. If we find anything which favours Arber's solution, we
are at liberty to accept it, in spite of Dr. Ames' dogmatic assertions
to the contrary.

[1] This is very near indeed to a buckle, in the sense used by
Arber.

[2] For the opposite opinion that the clamp was put on when the
barn was built or later *vide infra*.

THE CRACKED BEAM OF THE SHIP

[*To face p.* 14

speaks, was not let into the beam at all : it was used to raise the bending beam and bring it back into position, and would be removed as soon as the upright post was in its place. In other words it was a screw-press or screw-jack : probably all that was left of Brewster's printing house, after the types had been seized by the Leyden authorities. It has often perplexed one to find out why the passengers should have a great iron screw with them ; some of the books which record the incident speak of a passenger with a screw,[1] but that is not what Bradford said, nor what he reports the shipmen as saying. The supposition that it was a part of the old printing press makes it all clear. The printing house was broken up before they left Holland. The Leyden officials had taken the types away and prevented further complications from that quarter with the British Government. Brewer, who was the financial head of the printing-house, was gone to England, there to spend the greater part of his life in the Bishops' prisons ; Reynolds, the assistant, had retreated to Amsterdam ; Brewster and Winslow are on board the "Mayflower". They are the chief printers (Winslow being probably Brewster's master in the art), and we can quite understand how they came to pack up the remains of their machinery and take it with them to America. No doubt they designed to print more books, in days to come, in defence of their faith. They may have had a due sense of the truth that the Press is the lever that moves the world ; they certainly never suspected that the lever was going to be applied in a visible manner to keep a ship from foundering. The Press had become a Providence, like so many other things in the Pilgrim story.

[1] So Prince, apparently quoting Bradford : "A passenger having brought a great iron screw out of Holland".

CHAPTER V.

WHEN WAS THE SHIP BROKEN UP?

WE now come to the question as to the date when the barn was built, that is, the date when the loads of ship's timber were brought from the Thames waterside to Jordans. As there does not appear to be any date upon the building, we are obliged to transfer our attention to the farm-house to which it belongs, and to the documentary history of its ownership. If the barn was built at the same time as the oldest part of the farm-house, or nearly at the same time, the question of date can be settled at once ; otherwise it will remain unsettled, and challenge further investigation.

The visitor to the old farm kitchen, where the Quaker meetings were held in the middle of the seventeenth century, will be quick to notice the fine old fireplace and the adjacent ovens, all or nearly all the rest of the building appears to be modern. In the middle of the fireplace and at the back of it is a large iron plate, containing the royal arms. It has been restored to the fireplace where it evidently formerly belonged.[1] It was lying about in the neighbourhood of the farm-house when the Friends came into possession.

Here is a picture of the iron plate.

At a glance you can see that this is King James the First's coat-of-arms. It has Scotland quartered on it, for the first time and France, for not quite the last time. If one has any doubt on the point, look in Burke's *Peerage*, and you will see the very same arrangement of the lilies and leopards, etc. But there need be no doubt on the point ; for the date is here 16—18. So the old

---

[1] Or perhaps it belonged to another fireplace in an adjacent room, which fireplace is now bricked up.

IRON FIRE-PLATE WITH ROYAL ARMS

[*To face p.* 16

farm-house, i.e. the earliest part of it, was built, or re-built, in 1618. It appears to have been a royal posses-sion, or at least occupied by some one in close relation with King James, so as to act as his representative,[1] If then the barn was built at the same time, or nearly so, as the old farm-house, then the " Mayflower " (if it really was the " Mayflower ") was broken up after the death of Christopher Jones, in accordance with Mr. Marsden's theory. And in that case the " Mayflower " which re-placed her was the one that Moore and Child built at Aldborough, which passed almost at once into the hands of Mr. Thomas Horth of Yarmouth.

But how can we be certain that the barn is co-eval with the farm ? Perhaps the title-deeds may help us. The farm itself was owned in 1671 by a Quaker farmer of the name of William Russell. In that year he sold to Friends (Thomas Ellwood was one of them), for the sum of £4 2s. 6d. a piece of land to serve as a burial ground ; this is the present Quaker Place of Peace : (Russell's own daughter was the first to be laid there). It does not include the Meeting-House, which was built in 1688, on a piece of additional land, four acres in ex-tent, for which Friends gave the sum of £40. William Russell, who sold it to them, was the son of him that sold the graveyard, and the heir to his father's estate. Returning to the first vendor, we find that he was im-prisoned and distrained upon in 1676, for non-payment of tithes, at which time he was " near eighty and almost blind ". Ellwood and others went to prison with him. If, then, William Russell was almost eighty in the year 1676, it is reasonable to suppose that he had been in

[1] This splendid piece of iron-work can hardly have been designed by or for a yeoman farmer.

possession of the farm for many years.[1] So far nothing has been brought forward which would forbid the opinion that Russell had himself built the farm and the great barn. But we must not travel too fast, or we may overrun the scent. A reference to the Parish Registers of Chalfont St. Giles will tell us that

William Russell and Cicely Redinge, maryed at
London   3 July 1623.

The reason for recording the marriage at Chalfont is that it is a parish event : William Russell brought his wife home, apparently from London, in 1623. At that time it is reasonable to suppose he was in possession of the farm-house, and about twenty-six years of age. A possible objection may be made that perhaps he brought his wife to some other farm-house, and that he may have acquired Jordans at a later date. This is possible, but not at first sight likely ; we can, if we please, reserve judgment on the details of Mr. Russell's settlement : he was certainly a parishioner in 1623, or his marriage would not have been recorded.[2]

[1] He was born in 1600 and died in 1683.

[2] The Redinge family are also of the Parish: e.g. we have the following marriages :—

Wm. Basse and Luce Redinge,	15 July 1588.
John Wilde and Katherine Redinge,	9 Sep. 1588.
Thos. Redinge and Eliz. Dontoun,	29 Nov. 1591.
Xpofer Redinge (of Farnam Royall) and widow Redinge,	8 May 1599.
Jerome West and Suzanna Redinge,	14 Oct. 1602.
Wm. Wilkinson and Em. Reding,	6 Apr. 1618.
Wm. Widmore and Christian Reading,	20 Jan. 1618/19
Hy. Sams Jr. and Eliz. Reddinge (Lond.)	21 Oct. 1624.
Roger Maior, Gent. and Hester Reddinge, w[idow]	21 Oct. 1624.
Wm. Reading of Seare Greene and Amy Reading	21 July 1625.

Let us turn now to the barn and to its brick foundations. These foundations are made of courses of red
brick, and the size of each brick is 8¾ × 4¼ × 2⅜ inches.
Brickmaking is a somewhat late development in British
industries ; it had disappeared with the Romans, and
when it re-appeared in the Middle Ages, the supply in the
brick market was mostly Dutch and continental. Towards the end of Elizabeth's reign, building with brick
was becoming a common art, and its manufacture a
national industry, and it passed, like the rest of our national
life, under the control of Government and Guild.

On 11 February, 1620, the Justices of Middlesex
acquainted the bricklayers in and near London of the
order of the Lords of the Council respecting the manufacture of bricks, and we observe that the brick was to
be made of a standard size ; it was to be 9 inches long
by 4¼ in breadth and 2¼ in thickness, and the bricks
were to be sold at the price of 8s. a 1000 at the kiln.[1]

On 7 November, 1622, the Lords of the Council
make further regulations for brick-making, and a
Royal Proclamation is issued on the subject. The
Council say that the beauty and conveniency of brick-
building is now generally acknowledged ; so directions
must be given for the good and true making of bricks,
the size is to be 9 × 4⅜ × 2¼ inches, and the maximum
price of the controlled industry is to be 8s. the 1000 at the
kiln.[2] The Proclamation which accompanies the regula-

---

[1] *Calendar of State Papers*, S.P. Dom., cxii. : the *Calendar* says
2 × 4 × 2 inches, but this is a series of blunders. It should be as
we have written.

The reason why we have a 9-inch standard is to subdivide the
yard measure ; and the natural division of such a length should be
4¼ and 2¼ inches.

[2] S.P. Dom., vol. cxxxiv.

tion is illuminating : it is a Proclamation for the due making and sizing of Brick. Timber is declared to be scarce in England and is wanted for the Navy : so scarce has oak become that in London they are forced to use beech. Brick is a much better material, and reflects great credit on the city that builds with it. After 30 November, 1622, no one is to bring within five miles of the city bricks that are not made according to the following regulations. In particular all burnt bricks are to be nine inches long, four inches and a quarter and a half a quarter broad, and two inches and a quarter thick.[1] And such bricks are to be sold at the "Kill" for not more than 8s. the 1000.[2]

On the 2nd of May, 1625, a further Proclamation was issued concerning Buildings and Inmates within the City of London and the Confines of the same ; the orders of James and Elizabeth are referred to, and regulations are issued for the time of the year when brick-making is allowed and for the general processes of manufacture.[3]

On 16 July, 1630, another Proclamation was issued concerning new buildings in and about the City, etc. The Proclamation included regulations for making and

[1] I.e. 9 × 4⅜ × 2¼ inches. The *Oxford Dict.* says that the dimensions of an ordinary brick are 9 × 4⅜ × 2⅝ inches, but that the thickness varies from 3⅛ (as in Birmingham) to 1¾ inches.

[2] For this proclamation see *Mus. Britt.* 506, p. 12 (103) or the original signed copy in the *Record Office*, P.S.B., 1955.

[3] *Mus. Britt.* 506, p. 11 (40) and *Record Office*, P.S. 43.

This must be the document referred to in the *Encycl. Britannica*, where it is said that "the bricks made in England before 1625 were of many sizes, there being no recognised standard; but in that year the sizes were regulated by statute, and the present standard was adopted, viz. 9 × 4½ × 3 inches". The statement does not appear to be quite correct.

pricing bricks. The size of bricks when burned was to be 9 × 4⅜ × 2¼ inches, and the price 8s. per 1000 at the kiln, as in the previous Proclamation to which reference is officially made.[1] The standard brick, then, for London and the vicinity was 9 × 4⅜ × 2¼ inches. In 1724 an *Order of Tilers' and Brickl. Comp.* in the *London Gazette* (No. 6251/3) requires every brick to be 9 × 4¼ × 2¼ inches.[2]

When we compare the controlled sizes of bricks in the seventeenth century with those of the bricks in the Jordans Barn, it seems clear that these latter do not correspond to the control. They are irregular in dimension. Two explanations suggest themselves of the discrepancy. One is that the bricks are earlier in date than the operating control, in which case they should have been manufactured quite early in the seventeenth century : the other that they are imported bricks, say from Holland, which have not come under control. It will be seen from the foregoing Proclamations that by the end of November, 1622, such imported brick was prohibited in the London area unless it conformed to the City standard. Strictly speaking the regulations would not apply at first to the Buckinghamshire buildings, but after a time we may take it as certain that the standard of brick-makers in the Home Counties would conform to the London measurements. There is no sign of such conformity in the Jordans brick. This suggests an early date for the foundations of the

[1] This Proclamation may be found in *Mus. Britt.* 506, p. 11 (137) and the signed original in the *Record Office*, P.S., 153.

[2] The natural measure of a brick, as we have said, would be 9 × 4½ × 2½ inches, so as to allow for half-bricks and quarter-bricks by a change of position.

barn and for the break up of the ship. Shall we say, as early as 1625?

CHAPTER VI.

AN EXPERT'S OPINION.

IN order to test the accuracy of our judgment with regard to the structure of the old barn at Jordans and its relation to naval architecture, I secured the opinion of a Thames shipbuilder, of the first rank experimentally, asking him to advise me whether the building was built of ship's timber, without any reference to the " Mayflower " problem. He spent a part of a day in the examination of the building and reported to me as follows :—

" DEAR DOCTOR,

"As instructed I attended on the 16th April, 1920, at Jordans Hostel, Seer Green Halt, Bucks., for the purpose of inspecting the timber construction of the Barn adjoining same, and beg to report as follows :—

" ' The Barn was built in my opinion more than two hundred years ago, and is constructed of old ships' beams and frames.

" ' These I find in beautiful preservation.

" ' The timber uprights that support the roof are bilge timbers of a schooner : the plate on which the building rests and the sill are of the same class of timber split through.

" ' These have the original treenails and holes through which oak pegs were driven to fasten the timbers to the bottom planking of the vessel : these holes are $1\frac{1}{8}$ [inches] in diameter.

" ' The main supports to the roof are the cambered beams of a ship, and are fitted to the uprights in a fine workmanlike manner, all the fastening being wooden pegs throughout the building. The hundreds of perlines in the roof were cut from the side frames or uprights in the ship. I noticed that one of the sill timbers was part of the keelson of the vessel, as it still shows the marks of the side timbers to which this part was fastened with the treenail holes in same. The timbers or frames of the ship must have been 12 [feet] apart.

" ' On one of the uprights is a piece of convex iron band with square holes in same, which apparently is part of the stem band.

" ' The dimensions of the Schooner I estimate according to the size of the timber as being about 90 ft. long 22 ft. wide and 10 ft. deep, and would carry about 150 tons.

" ' In conclusion, the construction is beautiful to the nautical eye, as the building, if it were possible to turn same upside down, would resemble a timber-built ship.

" ' In the workmanship I noticed that shipwrights, or men who were connected with the craft must have built same, as many of the Tennons and Dovetails that join the timbers together are the work of skilled shipwrights.

" ' I must add that it has been a pleasure to me to give you this report.

" Joseph Hyams
" (Marine Surveyor).

" Blackwall Lane,
" East Greenwich."

The foregoing report may be taken as final confirmation of our discovery that the barn was built out of the timber of a ship (or ships). In reply to further questions on my part, a brief supplementary report was added. I wished to know, whether the three cross-beams in the adjacent building, originally the farm-stables, but now the dormitory of the Hostel, were from the same source as that which supplied the barn. The importance of this question lies in the fact, that, if answered in the affirmative, we might have to imagine a somewhat larger ship than Mr. Hyams had estimated.[1]

I also drew his attention to the clamped beam in the middle of the barn, in order to find out whether it had been cracked before the barn was built, or whether the clamp had been inserted at the time of building as a preventive against a possible collapse of the beam.

To these enquiries Mr. Hyams replied as follows :—

26/4/20.

"The crack in the beam referred to is a natural 'wind-shake,' and is found in oak trees where the branches shoot from in the form of a knot. The iron clamp on the same is a preventative from its going any further along the beam and so causing it to break in two. It must have been put on at the time of the construction of the barn.

"You are perfectly in order when you state that the same ship's timbers are used in the Hostel stables which we inspected.

"Yours faithfully,
"JOSEPH HYAMS.

"Blackwall Lane,
"East Greenwich."

It will be seen from the foregoing that the ship may have been somewhat larger than the first estimate ; it would certainly approximate closely to the traditional

---

[1] This is not a necessary, but only a possible consequence : the dormitory beams need not be regarded as a prolongation of the ship.

180 tons of the historic Mayflower. In fact, this tonnage is probably arrived at roughly by multiplying together a length of 90 ft. by a breadth of 20 ft. and a depth of 10 ft., and allowing 100 cubic ft. to the ton, and must be regarded as an approximation. Mr. Hyams does not think the beam had really been cracked before being used for the building; and in support of his belief that the clamp was put on at the time of building and as a precautionary measure, he pointed out to me that in the supporting joist a small piece of wood had been cut away, in order to expose one of the screw-heads. Thus his verdict was contrary to my opinion that the crack and the danger resulting therefrom were anterior to the building of the barn. His judgment was not affected, as mine might well have been, by a knowledge of the incident in Bradford's *Journal.* No other beam, however, in the building, even if cracked, shows signs of similar precautionary clamping; but, in view of the expert's opinion, we must not too hastily identify the cross-beam of the barn with the great beam amidships in the "Mayflower".

CHAPTER VII.

A Fresh Trail Struck.

A FURTHER examination of the farm buildings raises the question whether there are not traces in the oldest part of the woodwork of actual representations of the flower after which the famous ship was named. As we have said, very little remains in the farm-house itself that can be called ancient, except the fireplace and bake-ovens and, perhaps, some of the beams in the immediate neighbourhood.[1] There is, however, an old door,

---

[1] A second fireplace has apparently been bricked up and modernised.

to which my attention was drawn by my friend, Mr. Scott Duckers, covered with cross-pieces of roughly carved timber, of which the following is an exact representation.

These cross-pieces are adorned with carvings of what appears to be a rose ; a double wild-rose would perhaps be the nearest description. It does not appear to be the conventional Tudor rose ; indeed, in the year 1618 we should not expect to find that ; so the question is raised whether it may be a "Mayflower," and whether the door, wholly or in part, may not be ship's timber, as the great barn is, and, in that case, a Tudor rose might be possible.

One of the first questions asked will be a botanical one, what was, in the floral world, the "Mayflower" of which we are speaking? The next a nautical one : why are so many "Mayflowers" on the sea at this time? Taking the second question first, we may say that "Mayflower" stands for an original "Mary-flower" which has been displaced. We sometimes actually find it written "Mary-flower" in the records ; and sometimes we find, what appears to be a variant of the common form, a ship named "Mary Rose" or "Marygold". Thus the prevalence of Mayflower names may very well be a Catholic survival in the Mercantile Marine. The other question is harder to answer ; there is a multiplicity of May Flowers on land as well as at sea. The Hawthorn is the favourite flower of the Virgin, but we are not surprised to be told that there are May Lilies, and May Roses, and that in Devonshire the name is even given to the Lilac and to the Laurustinus,[1] while the Marigold with other flowers may also

---

[1] See Friend, *Flowers and Flower Lore*, ii. 472.

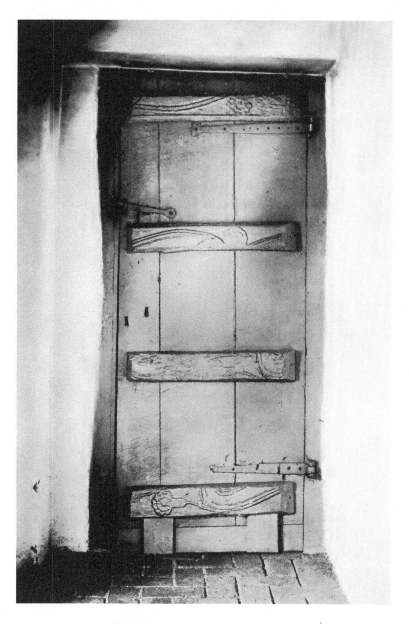

OLD DOOR WITH FLORAL CARVINGS.

[*To face p.* 26

claim recognition. We do not really need to decide the point as to which flower has the first claim to be called Flower of the May, or Flower of Mary : for our carving was not made for a herbal or a book of botany. It is clearly conventional, and there is nothing to prevent us from regarding it as a Mayflower. Apparently this is the only bit of carved work in the older parts of the farm buildings. That fact, alone, would be suggestive that the carving was symbolic. It stood for something in the place where it was first designed. If it came from a ship, say either the prow or the stern, or from the door of the chief cabin, we should expect, by analogy with modern nautical life, that the flower had something to do with the ship or her owners. She should be the Mayflower or the Mary Rose or the Marigold.

To Mr. Duckers, also, is due the important discovery, that the doorway of the farm encloses a second piece of the keel-iron of the ship.

This shows that the farm and the barn are built (or rebuilt) at the same time from the same materials. The date of the one is approximately the date of the other.

CHAPTER VIII.

A "MAYFLOWER" INSCRIPTION FOUND?

It was natural that special attention should be paid to the question of the existence of dates, inscriptions or other marks by which the Great Barn at Jordans could take its proper place in history. No such dates could however be found over any of the doorways, nor does there appear to be one on the small rough foundation stone at the S.W. angle. On examining the particular beams, there did not seem to be anything to note, except the Roman figures, or place-marks, cut on the beams to indicate where they were to be adjusted to some other beam similarly marked. There was, however, one cross-beam in the south wall, where I detected what looked like the remains of an incised inscription. In a favourable light, it seemed clear that there were remains of letters ; so I consulted my photographer, to whom this volume owes so much, to see whether by artificial light or by long exposure, the supposed script could be made visible. Being a man of very quick vision, he saw at once what I was after, and informed me that he could read it for me without a photograph ; and he proceeded to show that the inscription contained the following letters,

R. HARRIS,

and was a prophecy of my own name. This was certainly something like the introduction of Bill Stumps to his autograph. And the worst of the comedy was that the letters were very nearly as I had myself conjectured ; the last three were doubtful, but Mr. Muir was sure he could see a curve in the place where an S should occur. Comedy or Tragedy or Historical Play, there was nothing for it but to verify my autograph by scientific appliances. The picture which resulted is subjoined.

I can quite believe that most people will think we are operating in dream-land, and our inscribed autographs like ourselves, such stuff as dreams are made of. But I am confident this will not be the verdict of a trained epigraphist. He will certainly see some letters, if the light should be right, and will try to put them together. Was it possible that one of my own clan had been wood-carving on the beam? The answer must be negative; what is visible is a faint survival in a very old piece of timber ; a modern incision would

INCISED LETTERS ON BEAM

[To face p. 29

betray itself at once. If on the other hand it is as old, or nearly so, as the beam, what can be said further by way of reading or interpretation? Would it not be better to swallow one's perplexities and say nothing? The explanation which occurred to me, at a somewhat later date, of the mysterious alphabetic signs is as follows : the name which Mr. Muir read as Harris is correct as far as the letters go except for the fourth and sixth: we have then

HAR + I +.

Suppose we expand it as follows :

HAR[W]IC[H].

We have now the ship's port of registry ; and when that is settled, the ship's own name must precede; and we write

[MAYFLOWE]R. HAR[W]IC[H].

The beam is taken, apparently, from the stern of the ship, where we commonly find the name and the port. The ships of the period had high and square sterns.

Now we remember Mr. R. G. Marsden's discovery, of which he gave an account in the *English Historical Review*,[1] and to which I have made frequent reference in my book *The Last of the Mayflower*, that the ship in which the Pilgrims sailed was the "Mayflower of Harwich," and her captain and part-owner was Christopher Jones *of Harwich*.

It is surprising that we were able to read the letters ; the beam, as the photograph shows, is much decayed, and has probably suffered some abrasion, which would explain the disappearance of the rest of the name. If the beam had been turned in the other direction, I

[1] Vol. xix.

suppose no signs of lettering would have remained ; the weather would have removed them.   In the process of rebuilding the inscription was taken into the inside of the ship !   On closer investigation, I begin to be sceptical as to the letter R, which we have suggested to be terminal of the " Mayflower ".   Perhaps it is an illusion. In that case we must look for the traces of " Mayflower " on some similar beam in some other part of the building.   We have not yet found it.

CHAPTER IX.

WHO BROUGHT THE SHIP TO JORDANS?

MR. HYAMS' observation, that the barn was actually built by shipwrights, is of the first importance.   It is clear that the ship was bought entire, as she lay in her dock, or dismantled on the quay ; she did not come on the market as broken timber ; she was taken to pieces in such a way that she could be put together again, and the shipwrights came with the numbered and assorted beams to show how she might be reproduced in an inverted position, so far as that was possible.   Such a task would require time for its accomplishment.   It means that there was some connecting link between the Buckinghamshire country-side and the Thames water-side, which brought the reconstruction of the ship into the area of practical politics.   Where shall we find such a connecting link ? certainly not amongst the men of the wharf or the woodyard.   Their object would be to break the frame up as fast as hammers and axes could do the work, and get the money value of the woodpile at the earliest possible date.   The preservation of the ship must find its reason in the mind of its chief owner and financier.   The capitalist must be lurking somewhere

in the neighbourhood of the reconstructed ship : he must
be sought among the Puritans of Buckinghamshire, who
at that time were holding and playing the winning cards
in the great game of English Liberty. If, for example,
John Hampden, who actually visited the Plymouth
Colony in its early days, had heard that the old ship was
to be broken up, he might very well have said, " Let us
build a temple of Freedom with her beams, for they are
greatly to be had in reverence ". We have, however,
no evidence that Hampden took a part in the initial
venture, in such a way as to make a commemoration of
it on his part desirable. We have no reason to suppose
that he was one of the actual owners of the original
"Mayflower".[1] Is it possible that amongst these owners
there was a Buckinghamshire man from the immediate
neighbourhood of the Chalfonts? Let us see what we
know about them.

Mr. Marsden found among the *Acts of the High
Court of Admiralty*[2] the appraisement of the " Mayflower " in anticipation either of her dissolution or of a
change of ownership ; and he tells us that "about two
years after the death of Christopher Jones, on 4 May,
1624, Robert Childe, John Moore and [Joan] widow of
Christopher Jones, owners of three-fourths of the
'Mayflower,' obtained a decree in the Admiralty
Court for her appraisement. She was then, probably,

[1] The suggestion arises whether, in view of the fact that
Christopher Jones was a whaler, and his ship a whaling-ship, the
missing owner might not belong to the group of financiers who sent
ships to Greenland, such as Mr. Nathaniel Wright of London, or
Mr. Thomas Horth of Great Yarmouth. Wright, for instance, spent
many years in Biscay, and his absence from home might be the
reason for his non-appearance at the appraisement. But this is
pure conjecture, we do not as yet know the fourth owner.
[2] 30, f. 227.

lying in the Thames for the commission of appraisement issued to four mariners and shipwrights of Rotherhithe. The appraisement is extant. It is a significant document as regards her age and condition. . . . It is possible that the owner of the remaining one-fourth of the ship was unwilling to contribute to the cost of repairing her, or of fitting her out for a new voyage, and that the other co-owners took proceedings to compel him to contribute ; or possibly the appraisement was made to fix the value of the widow Joan Jones's one-fourth, etc."

Whatever be the explanation, the result of the appraisement is to remove the widow from the combination, and perhaps to reduce the ownership even further. We have found two of the owners, viz. Robert Child and John Moore. Of these two it seems that Child was the financial, and Moore the nautical expert, for it appears that Moore took command, at least for a time, of the new "Mayflower" that was laid down at Aldeburgh, probably under his own direction.

Is there any ground for connecting either of the two with Bucks or with the Chalfont area ? Anyone who is familiar with the village life of South Bucks will say that these are county names, and anyone who is familiar with the struggles of the Puritans or the Quakers of Bucks in the seventeenth century will confirm the verdict. As I am more familiar with the Quaker story in Bucks than with the Puritan communities amongst whom Quakerism burst into flower, I will show that the two names are both Quaker names, and that in particular the name of Child has great prominence for this part of the county.

Let us take an instance or two of what I mean. Thomas Ellwood closes his history abruptly in the year 1683, with the story of a raid made on the Quakers, when they were meeting at Wooburn in Bucks, by Sir Dennis Hampson of Taplow, in the commission of the peace, accompanied by a troop of horse ; twenty-three men were arrested and taken to Aylesbury Prison on a charge of riot. After some three months in prison, they were convicted of the riot, though, as Ellwood says, they were only sitting peaceably together, without word or action, and though there was no proclamation made, nor they required to depart. Ellwood closes his account, which can be expanded from Besse's *Sufferings of the Quakers* by giving the names of the criminals, and their appropriate sentences. (*Seventeen of them remained in prison until King James's proclamation of pardon in* 1686.) Among the names of the faithful company, we find Timothy Child, Robert Moore, and Edward Moore.

Somewhat later in the century, we find, amongst the persons prosecuted for tithes, and grossly plundered in consequence of their refusal to pay, the name of Henry Child, of Amersham. In the year 1698 the same Henry Child heads the testimony against John Robbins, who had brought dishonour on the Quaker name.[1] It even stands before John Penington and Thomas Ellwood ; we must not make too much of precedence, but he is clearly one of the Quaker pillars. The Child family of Amersham was come into the Quaker fold. Here is a fragment of a table of 385 burials in the Jordans graveyard between 1671 and 1845.

It will be seen at a glance that Child is one of the leading Quaker names in this district.

---

[1] The Testimony is headed :—

"From our monthly meeting holden at Hunger Hill [near Amersham] for the service of the Church of Christ in the Upper Side of the County of Bucks, this fifth day of the seventh month, 1698."

3

(The same table does not show a single Moore : the Quaker Moores do not belong to this area.)

Now let us look back to pre-Quaker days and see if we can find Robert Child. If he is a shipowner or shipbuilder in the early decades of the century, we should find him in the Amersham registers of the end of the sixteenth century. Here are some instances of the family name from the Marriage Records of the Parish of Amersham.

Johes Child & Elizabeth Treadway	4 Feb., 1571.
Johes Child & Margeria Weste	28 Sep., 1572.
Robert Childe & Johanna Horne	9 Feb., 1576.
Hy. Ball & Susanna Childe	10 Nov., 1583.
Wm. Childe & Isabella Nashe	7 Sep., 1584.
Robert Childe & Johanna Osborne	16 Nov., 1584.
Wm. Grimsdale & Edina Childe	8 Nov., 1585.
Wm. Childe & Johanna Hardinge	9 Oct., 1587.
Xpofer Clarke & Jana Childe	1 June, 1590.
Waterus Bell & Anna Childe	28 Sep., 1590.
Robert Childe & Margareta Batchiler	10 Feb., 1592.
Robert Childe & Johanna Haythorne	29 Sep., 1597.
Robert Childe & Eliz. Tylliarde	25 Oct., 1597.
Wm. Child & Eliz. Watkins	26 Sep., 1599.
Richard Grimsdall & Marie Child	16 July, 1604.

& so on.

No one can examine this register, without coming to the conclusion that the Child clan was strong in Amersham,[1] and that one of the family leaders was

[1] I have counted thirty-eight marriages of the Child clan in Amersham before 1700 : for High Wycombe, where the clan also is represented, there are nine marriages in the seventeenth century. In other places they occur sporadically.

...dly, Sarah 130 aged _ ...member ..._
d° William 1824, aged 76. Giles Chalfont. (a non-member).

C

Clapham Margery, 1693. The Dean, G Chalfont. Wife of Richard, a Tailor
  d° Richard, 1700. G Chalfont Tailor
Chawley Robert, 1705. G Chalfont Yeoman
Carter Alice, 1707. Wife of Samuel
Chawley Elizabeth, 1707. G Chalfont Widow
  d° Rebecca 1708. dau. of Joseph The Dean, G Chalfont
Cowley (or Coulsell?) Henry, 1710/11. Burnham, Bucks
Carol Elizabeth, 1713. Farnham
Chawley Joseph, 1720. The Dean G Chalfont. son of Joseph
Tirrell Mary, 1724. Rickmansworth
Child, Mary 1727. Infant (? dau. of Giles and Mary, of Hedgerley Dean)
Caleb William, 1730. The Cherry Trees Chesham
Child Sarah 1731. Wife of William
Coulsell, Giles, 1732.
Towdrey Sarah, 1732. Wife of Thomas, of Oak Mill, Iver, Bucks
Child Catharine, 1734. Wife of Timothy of Hedgerley Dean, Farnham Royal
Coulsell (or Colchill) Henry, 1736. Burnham
Child _____ 1737, son of Giles Hedgerley Dean, Farnham Royal
Coburton Mrs. 1741. Wife of Jonas of London, Cousin to Mary Barter
Coulsell Mrs 1742. Wife of John
  d° John, 1743.
Child Timothy, 1743. Hedgerley F Royal
Chawley, Joseph 1743. The Dean G Chalfont
Child Mary, 1749, dau. of William
  d° Jonas, 1744, wife of d°
Chapple Ruth, 1759. Iring, Herts (? if at Jordans)
Child Joseph, 1759. Burnham
  d° Giles, 1764. Hedgerley Dean, F Royal
Chawley Rebecca 1767. The Dean, G Chalfont
Child Mary, 1768. Hedgerley Dean, F Royal. Widow of Giles
  d° James 1770, son of James
Coburton Jonas 1776. London, Cutler
Chawley Robert, 1776. G Chalfont
Child Giles 1778. aged 19. F Royal, son of Timothy, a Wheeler, grandson to William
  d° William, 1779. aged 81. F Royal, a Wheelwright
Cowley, Mary Junior, 1785 aged 57. Oakmill, Bucks, dau. of Thomas and Mary
Child James, 1796. aged 64. Wapses, Bucks, Labourer (a non-member)

D

PART OF BURIAL REGISTER AT JORDANS

[To face p. 34

Robert Child, at the very time when we were enquiring into the ownership of the " Mayflower ". We need not spend further time over the matter ; it is a fair supposition that the chief owner of the " Mayflower " came from the very region where the great barn was, according to local tradition, built out of her bones. Thus the tradition would be verified at every point. The same records show that Robert Child was buried in 1649 ; as far as one can judge from the records, he was married three times and lived to an advanced age. But there may be some confusion between two people of the same name.

The identification of Robert Child should also help us to the date of the building of the barn. It cannot have been far on in the seventeenth century. Whoever paid for it, or erected it, whether one of the Gardiner family, or one of the Fleetwood family who have manorial rights over Jordans, or one of the Russell family, or some unknown person, the date of the appraisement determines the superior limit of time for the building. It was, therefore, put up not long after the summer, and perhaps in the summer of 1624. So that Mr. Marsden was right, and I was wrong ; he stood (with some reservation of judgment),[1] for two " Mayflowers," one of which might have replaced the other ; I inclined to a single long-lived ship, engaged constantly in Greenland and Biscay ventures with occasional voyages to New England.

[1] As stated above, he thought that the unknown fourth owner was perhaps unwilling to contribute to the repairs of the ship, and that the appraisement was intended to force him to contribute, *so that she might undertake a fresh voyage.* Evidently Mr. Marsden was doubtful as to what became of the "Mayflower ". The documents are not doubtful.

To make the position clearer, I have re-examined the documents relative to the appraisement, and find that there was no reason why Mr. Marsden should have hesitated, nor why I should have accepted the alternative of a transfer of the ship to other hands after appraisement. The records say positively that she was broken up, as the next chapter will show. Meanwhile the answer to the question at the head of the chapter is that the "Mayflower" was probably brought to Jordans by an agreement on the part of the owner of the farm with one of the owners of the ship, to wit, Robert Child.[1]

CHAPTER X.

The "Mayflower" Broken Up.

The papers which describe the appraisement of Christopher Jones' "Mayflower" are two in number. The first is an appeal in Latin to the Admiralty for an appraisement of the ship: the second is the report of the shipwrights and mariners to whom the appraisement was entrusted. We give the transcription of them in order.

[1] There is a possibility of finding Robert Child elsewhere. For instance, there was a Dr. Robert Child who came to New England twice, and who, with his brother, Major John Child, gets into a dispute with Winslow, and publishes a reply to his *Hypocrisie Unmasked.* But this was in 1647. Winslow replied to him in *New England's Salamander discovered.*

Then there is Robert Child, clothier, of Headington in Wilts, the father of Francis Child, the banker of Temple Bar. Francis was the first English banker; he was born in 1642. The curious thing is that the bank has still a Marigold on their cheques, and on their buildings. It is said that they annexed a public-house of that name, when they became bankers "with running cashes" instead of goldsmiths. It is an uncanny coincidence!

High Court of Admiralty
Stats., Vol. 30, fol. 227.

26 May, 1624.   Negocium appretiationis navis voca-
tae the "Mayflower" portus London
promotum per Robertum Childe
Johannem Moore et—Jones relic-
tam Christopheri Jones defuncti
proprietarios trium quartarum partium ejusdem navis.

                              WYAN.

Die predicto : [sc. 26 May, 1624] coram Edmundo
Pope legum doctore surrogato, etc., in camera sua, etc.
Presente me Thoma Wyan notario publico comparuit
Wyan et exhibuit procuratorium suum pro dictis parti-
bus promoventibus et fecit, etc. etc., et allegavit dictos
dominos suos esse proprietarios trium quartarum partium
dictae navis the "Mayflower," *eandemque navem in
ruinis esse,* quare ut valor ejusdem appareat petiit ean-
dem navem ejusque apparatus et accessiones auctoritate
hujus curiae appretiandam fore decerni.   Quod dominus
ad ejus petitionem decrevit.

From the foregoing it appears clearly that the ship
was already broken up (*in ruinis esse*).   Three of its
owners, Childe, Moore, and Widow Jones, make an
appeal through a notary public named Wyan for an
appraisement, which is officially conceded by the presid-
ing officer of the Court.

The appraisement comes back in an English document, as follows :—

High Court of Admiralty
Libels 81.   No. 167.

The appraisement or valuacion of the shippe the
"Mayflower" of London, and her tackle and furniture,

taken and made by aucthoritye of His Majesty's highe courte of Admiraltye the 26th day of May, 1624, at the instance of Roberte Childe, John Moore and —— Jones, the relict of Christopher Jones deceased, owners of three fowerth partes of the said shippe, by us William Craford and Francis Birkes of Redriffe,[1] Marriners, Robert Clay and Christopher Malym of the same, shippwrightes as followeth :—

In primis wee the said appraisers having viewed and seene the Hull, mastes yardes boate Winles [2] and capstan of and belonging to the said shipp, Doe estimate the same at	l^{li} (i.e. £50).
Item five anckors weighinge about 25 cwt. wee value at	xxv^{li} (i.e. £25).
Item one suite of sailes more then half worne, we estimate at	xv^{li} (i.e. £15).
Item 3 cables, 2 hawsers, the shrowdes and stayes with all the other rigginge more than half worne, at	xxxv^{li} (i.e. £35).
Item 8 muskettes, 6 bandeleers and 6 pikes at	l^{s} (i.e. £2 10s.)]
Item ye pitch pott and kettle	xiii^{s} 4^{d}
Item ten shovells	v^{s}

Summa totalis

128^{li} 08^{s} 04^{d}
(i.e. £128 8 4).

[1] I.e. Rotherhithe.
[2] Windlass.

In witnes whereof wee the said appraisers have hereunto putt our handes

FRAUNCES BIRKS.

WM. CRAIFORD.

ROBART CLAYE.

CHRISTOPHER MALIM.

It will be seen that the valuation is much less than Mr. Marsden supposed (he says £160) and so we see again that it must be the break-up price. There is no hint that it is the widow's fourth. The price, as well as the statement that the ship was *in ruinis*, excludes the idea, which we at first patronised, that she was to pass, after appraisement, into other hands. As she was already broken up, we must conclude that she was used for building in the summer of 1624, and this date agrees very well with the time of building of the farm and its attached out-buildings, as well as with the character of the bricks employed in the substructure; and since the barn has been shown to be the work of shipwrights and not of local builders and carpenters, the probability is that the workmen who took her to pieces at Rother-hithe were employed at Jordans in her reconstruction. Her chief owner and final purchaser must have been somewhere in the Jordans area.

CHAPTER XI

THE OWNERS OF THE JORDANS FARM.

WE come now to a difficult question, the identification of the owner of the farm in the years 1618-24 when the farm buildings and the attached barns appear to have been erected. We showed that the Friends' Burial Ground was acquired from an old man named

William Russell in the year 1671.[1] There was no *a priori* reason against his having been the owner in 1624; we found his marriage in 1623; but *a priori* reasonings as to ownership of property are not of the nature of evidence; and we have to turn to legal records in search of the actual proprietor, or occupier at the date in question.

The name *Jordans farm* comes down out of the old time, when some one of the name of Jordan was in possession. The name appears in an Inquisition *post-mortem* made on 21 January, 33 Henry VIII. [= 1541/2] at Colnbrook before Paul Darrell, esq., escheator.[2]

The jurors [named] say that William Gardyner was seised of the manor of Grove Place, Bucks, and of 9 crofts called Wellers in Chalfont St. Giles and a messuage with appurtenances called Groves Meese there *alias* Jurdany, and parcels of land . . . belonging to the said manor from old time, etc. Grove Place and other premises in Chalfont St. Peter and Chalfont St. Giles are held of Edward Restwold, esq., of his manor of Le Vache, etc.

This is the first suggestion we found of the name of Jordan, in connection with the property.[3] The name Jordan, as a personal name, can be traced in

[1] The Episcopal Returns for 1669 report that there is in Chalfont St. Giles, *in the house of William Russell*, a meeting of Quakers, 60 or 70 in number, of inconsiderable quality, with Isaac Penington for their Teacher.

[2] Public Record Office, *Chancery Series* ii., vol. 64, No. 96. Mrs. Sefton Jones has traced the name for several centuries earlier.

[3] In the researches that involve the Record Office, Somerset House, etc., I am greatly indebted for the help and advice of Mr. Edward Salisbury, of the Record Office, and his sister, Miss Edith Salisbury.

various parishes of South Bucks in the following century.

Our next piece of evidence is more important, as it appears to show that in the year 1635-6 tax was levied on Chalfont St. Giles in the name of the King, and a dispute arose as to whether Jordans Farm, stated to be in the occupation of *Thomas* Russell, but owned by a member of the Gardiner family, was subject to the tax in question. As the document is important for our purposes, we go into the matter at some length. It is a case of

Exchequer Depositions by Commission
(12 Car. I. No. 35 Bucks).

The writ is dated 12 February, 11 Charles I. [= 1635/6]. Interrogatories are made of Anthony Radcliffe *esq.* as plaintiff against Hen. Sames sen., Hen. Sames jr. and Thomas Russell, gent., as defendants.

The following questions are asked :—

1. Do you knowe of any Taxe or certaynty issuing yearly to his ma^{tie} out of the village of Chalfont St. Giles?

2. How has it been collected?

3. Have the inhabitants rated the same among themselves?

4. Do you know that one Gardiner was owner of a tenement called the Grove in the said parishe, and of Jordans Farme in the same parishe and of the house the plaintiff now dwells in?

5. What rate did Gardiner pay?

6. Of what value are those tenements?

7. Have the defendants refused to pay the tax?

8. Have divers poor inhabitants been distrained to pay the whole tax?

9. Has plaintiff been threatened by the sheriff with distraint for the whole tax?

'This list of questions is answered on behalf of the plaintiff and then on behalf of the defendants by various parishioners. The important thing for us is that Gardiner is said to be the owner of the properties referred to ; Radcliffe the plaintiff occupies the Stone Farm, the Sames family occupy the Grove, and Thomas Russell occupies Jordans Farm.

It appears that Jordans Farm is not yet in possession of the Russell family, though occupied by Thomas Russell. The evidence is that it still belongs to the Gardiner family. The King has some rights of taxation, but the defendants refuse to pay, and the rest of the parish cannot agree on the subdivision of the rating. The witnesses affirm that they never heard that the tax in question was levied on the Grove or on Jordans.

This interesting document which is too long for further quotation gives us an idea of the ownership of the property in 1636. In the course of the enquiry William Russell, of Chalfont St. Giles, yeoman, aged 59, gave evidence, and in answer to the second question, stated that "certaine houses doe pay and certaine houses do not pay towards the said certainty"; he paid 2s. when it was demanded thirty years since. This cannot be the William Russell who sold the graveyard to the Friends, but some one of an earlier generation, perhaps the father of our William Russell. He does not say on what property he paid the tax in 1606.

We conclude that Jordans Farm was in the occupation of the Russell family some time before 1636, but that they became owners of it at a later date. The reversion of the property at this date is said to belong to one John Gardiner.

Certainly this suggests that the Gardiner family had been in possession since A.D. 1541/2 as we found out by the previous Inquisition. But here is another Inquisition made in the first year of Elizabeth, 1558/9, which says the same thing.

Inquisitio post-mortem.
(1 Eliz., C. series ii., vol. 118, No. 3)
William Gardiner.
1558/9. Inquisition taken at Whadsdon, 4 January, 1 Eliz., before Edmund Windsor and John Christopher.

The Jurors say that William Gardyner was seised [*inter alia*] of the manor of Grove Place, Bucks, 9 crofts called Wellders in Chalfont St. Giles, a messuage called Groves Mees *otherwise Jordans*, etc.

Part of his will is recited, bequeathing the manor of Grove Place, with its appurtenances, to Anne his wife, for life, etc. He died 13 October, 1558, leaving John his son and heir, aged 11 years on 19 September, 1558.

Thus the Gardiner family are in possession from A.D. 1541, to A.D. 1636 (at least), and it is probably from them that the Russell family acquired the farm of which they had previously been occupiers. It is very likely that the manor rolls of the manor of the Vache, which includes the manor of Grove Place, would tell us definitely when the farm was transferred. But this is not of immediate importance. The point ascertained is that the Russell family passed from being tenants to actual ownership somewhere about the middle of the seventeenth century. This result is entirely independent of the hypothesis that Robert Child and perhaps John Moore were Buckinghamshire men. It would not be affected if they should turn up in the registers at

Harwich or Aldeburgh.[1] The case for a Bucks origin of Robert Child is, however, very strong.

As to John Moore, we find that he was designated master of the new ship "Mayflower," built in 1625 by Robert Child, John Totten, Michael (or Myles) White, and others. This makes it more probable that his home was on the waterside, either on the Thames or in Suffolk, than that he was a financier, hailing from Bucks, and perhaps operating in London. It also raises the question whether the missing fourth owner of the original ship may not have been either Totten or White: on this point we are still in the dark, and must not make hasty suggestions, or anticipate conclusions which may be arrived at by closer investigation.

It would not in the least surprise me, if it should turn out that some one from this part of Buckinghamshire had actually joined the Pilgrims, and been amongst those who are denominated First Comers. One naturally looks for a Child or a Russell, but they do not appear. Here is a curious coincidence which may deserve some consideration.

A part of the hill that overlooks the harbour of New Plymouth is known as Coles' Hill. It is described as follows in the *Notes on Plymouth, Mass.* in *Mass. Hist. Soc. Collections*, ser. ii., 3, 179.

"Cole's Hill, an open green, and pleasant spot, in Plymouth, well-known, fronting the harbour, is the

---

[1] Mr. Arthur J. Winn shows conclusively that they are not Aldeburgh names. In the *East Anglian Times* for 17 June, 1920, he states that he has searched for the families of Christopher Jones and his friends in the Aldeburgh Church Register from 1580 to 1600, and can find no trace of them ; nor do the registers of neighbouring villages give any better result: "no more mention of Christopher Jones and his friends than of Christopher Columbus," says Mr. Winn.

place where it is said the dead were buried who died the first winter, 1620."

To which Justin Winsor (*Hist.* iii. 273 *n.*) adds that it perpetuates the name of one of the early comers, Stephen (?) Coale.

Bartlett, *Pilgrim Fathers*, describes the situation as follows : " From Leyden Street we descend rather steeply into another, which runs parallel with the sea-shore, and leads to the famous Forefather's Rock. On our left is an abrupt ridge, the top of which is open, and covered with grass, but its sides disguised by modern edifices. This is called Cole's Hill, and was the original burial-place of the Pilgrims during the dreadful mortality of the first winter."

Justin Winsor treats it as a name of local ownership. It will be difficult to establish this. Coale is not one of the First Comers. On the other hand it may very well be, like so many other names in the district, a transplanted English name.

If we start to walk from Amersham towards Jordans, through the Child-Russell country, we shall pass first the Child woods, and then, one mile from Amersham, the hill and hamlet and green that bears the name of Coleshill. Close by is Ellwood's house, at Hunger [Ongar] Hill, where for many years the Friends' meetings used to be held alternately with Jordans. It would be quite easy for an emigrant from this area to transplant the name of Coleshill with him. But the proof of such a transfer is not forthcoming.

Can we go any further in the search for a " Mayflower " man in the district where our enquiries have been prosecuted? It is clear that amongst the First Comers of the Colony, there is no one named Child and no one named Russell. But, since neither Child nor

Russell actually owned, at this time, the Jordans farm, the question arises naturally whether there may not have been a Gardiner among the Pilgrims? The answer is prompt in the affirmative ; Richard Gardiner signed the compact in the cabin of the " Mayflower " at Cape Cod ; he had an acre of land assigned to him at the first allotment in 1623 ; and, to show that he is not an insignificant person, he writes a preface in 1622 to the book called *Mourt's Relation*, which is signed R. G. and addressed to the head of the " Mayflower " adventure, Master John Pierce. Nothing more is known of him, except that Bradford tells us, at the end of his *Journal*, that he became a seaman and died, either in England or at sea. Here, then, is our missing link found ; the Gardiner family are implicated in the Great Adventure. We knew that some of the clan belonged to the early Nonconformists, for there was a John Gardiner who was a Protestant recusant in the twenty-ninth year of Elizabeth (A.D. 1587), and again in the thirty-fourth year of Elizabeth (A.D. 1592). He is described as being of Filmer, which is only a short distance to the south of the Chalfonts and he must belong to the same family as owned the Jordans farm. We will see whether we find Richard Gardiner in the local registers, or if we can find anything more about the Gardiner clan which may connect them with the " Mayflower ".[1]

[1] Dr. Whitley reminds me that four children of the name of More were sent out in the " Mayflower ". Three of them died the first winter. Is it possible that they are connected with Thomas Moore, who would thus be personally involved in the Adventure, as the Gardiner family were?

CHAPTER XII

THE FOURTH OWNER OF THE "MAYFLOWER" FOUND.

WE have shown in what precedes that the Jordans farm with its attached ship-built barn was the property of the Gardiner family, and that it passed from them to the Russell family at some time in the middle of the seventeenth century; and we have suggested that there may have been some connection between the Gardiner clan and a certain Richard Gardiner who sailed in the "Mayflower". At this point we find ourselves in difficulties; for the name Gardiner is a common one, but the Gardiner clan, whom we have been detecting among the owners of Jordans farm, does not crop up in the Chalfonts, in the same way as the Child clan does in the district round Amersham. We must go outside the county in search of their ancestry.

We showed in the previous chapter from an inquisition made on 21 January, 1541/2 that William Gardyner was at his death the owner of the Manor of Grove Place and, amongst other properties, of the Jordans farm. Let us, then, see if we can find his will. To do this, we go to Somerset House. Here is an abstract of the document desired :—

Somerset House, P.C.C. (i.e. Prerogative Court of Canterbury).

Will of William Gardyner, 1542 (4 Spert).
Will of William Gardyner, of Grove Place, Bucks.
Wife = Cicely.
Sons = William, John, Edmond, Edward.
Daughters = Mary, Christian, Alice, Elizabeth.
Residuary legatee = eldest son William.

Testator was a freeman of the city of London, but forsook that freedom more than twenty years past. Refers to "my dwelling-house in Bucklers Bery of London," purchased of—Woodcok, and now bequeathed to my wife Cicely.

Also "my house in Bucklersbury of London, called the catt and the fydell" bequeathed to my second son John.

Two houses in Buggerowe, London, bequeathed to sons Edward and Edmond.

Executors : wife and eldest son.

Overseers : Will Mery, grocer ; John Duffilde, brewer ; Henry Polsted, gent.

Witnesses : Henry Polsted, Thos. Thacker.

Dated : 18 Apr. 1541.

Proved : 12 Apr. 1542.

The will shows conclusively that Gardiner was a Londoner, living in Bucklersbury (for which, and its sweet scent in "simpling time," see Shakespeare). There is no mention here of Jordans or the Bucks property, but these are involved in the *Inquisition* of the previous chapter, made between the death of the testator and the probate of his will.

Our next step must be to find the will of William Gardiner, the eldest son.

We referred in the previous chapter to the *Inquisition* made after his death on 4 January, 1558/9. His will is in Somerset House (P.C.C. 36 Loftes), and the following is an abstract :—

William Gardiner, 1561.

Will of William Gardiner, esq., of Grove Place, Chalfont St. Giles, Bucks, dated 3 Oct. 1558.

Wife = Anne.

Sons = John the eldest, William, Thomas, Robert.

Daughters = Frances, Anne, Margaret, Awdrye.

Father = William Gardiner, deceased whose executor the testator is.

Sisters = Elizabeth Gardiner,—Stanbridge,—Godolphin.

Ward = Sybell Newdegate, niece of Sybell Newdegate, gentlewoman, deceased.

Brothers = John Newdigate, Frances Newdigate, and James Bacon, William Godolphin, Brothers- John Gardiner, Thomas Newdegate, in-law Antony Newdegate, Nicholas Newdegate, Robt. Newdegate.

Cousin = Richard Crayford, to whom the testator sold woods in Fulmer.

Another cousin = " My ladie Perryn ".

Executors : John Newdigate, esq., Master Will. Godolphin, James Bacon, citizen and fishmonger of London ; brother John Gardiner, citizen and grocer of London ; and wife.

Overseers : Rich. Crayforde, esq. ; friend Thomas Ball, of Beaconsfield, and servant John Greene.

Bequeaths the Manor of Grove Place, and all other lands in parish of Chalfont St. Giles, to his wife, except the lease of Sylvesden, Sylvesden Crofte and Dorsettes Farme, which go to son John. Other lands are mentioned in co. Oxford.

Witnesses ; John Newdegate, Edward Baber, Thomas Newdigate, John Gardiner, Will. Godolphin, John Greene.

Date of Probate : 26 Nov. 1561.

The foregoing document shows that the family emerged from London life, and acquired county possessions, not far from the city where their wealth was accumulated. There is no trace here of a Richard Gardiner. For our enquiry the most important thing which comes to light from this will is the relationship of the Gardiners to the Crayford family. Richard Crayforde, esq., is stated to be William Gardiner's cousin, and to have bought from him woods in Filmer (the next parish to the Chalfonts on the south). The two families are adjacent landowners in Bucks. Now we notice that although the name of Gardiner is common enough, the name of Crayford is by no means usual; and we are struck by the fact that *it is the name of one of the appraisers of the "Mayflower" in* 1624. The coincidence is so peculiar that we have to go back to the document of the appraisement and see what it means. Is there any connection genealogically or otherwise between Richard Crayforde, esq., in 1561 and Wm. Craiford, mariner, in 1624?

The appraisement was made on behalf of four owners of the ship, three of whom are coercing the fourth (unless he should be absent and out of reach): and there are four appraisers, of whom each one naturally represents an owner and looks after his interest. Mr. Marsden's idea was that the anonymous owner was being coerced by the other three to pay his share of the refitment of the ship for a further voyage, and that the break-up or transfer of the ship was due to his refusal to find his share of the funds. This is not at all likely; one of the owners, the widow Jones, was not the person to be spending her money patching up the ship, and the same thing is true of Moore the mariner. If there has been coercion, it must have been attempted by the anonymous person, who has wished to send the " Mayflower" to sea again, after a complete overhauling, and cannot persuade his co-owners to co-operate. They have settled the matter by breaking up the ship and demanding a valuation of her materials. Suppose we say that the fourth owner was Gardiner, and that Crayford is his nominee on the appraisement (as being his kinsman), we can then explain the whole transaction, the purchase of the ship and its immediate transfer to the Jordans farm. Three of the owners were bought out on a forced sale and valuation by the fourth, who may even have secured an option on the broken-up materials. Gardiner bought the ship, because he was part-owner, and one of the appraisers was a distant relation of his. He bought it, as far as we can judge, at a very modest price. When I first saw the valuation, as given by Mr. Marsden at £160, and noted his remark that it was only one-fourth of her value, I suggested that the valuation was merely for probate and for the widow's fourth part ; but the price is much less than Mr. Marsden's figure, and is given in the document as just over £128, and it is clear that the ship was dismantled, and not merely her value redistributed.

The position that we have now reached is this : that somewhere before 1625, Gardiner, the owner of the Jordans farm, built a new farm-house and a new barn, employing for that purpose the timbers of a dismantled ship ; and that, in the year 1624, one of the appraisers of the broken-up ship "Mayflower," was a Crayford, who appears to belong to a family of that name, which is closely connected with the Gardiners of Chalfont St. Giles, and who are adjacent landowners to them. The natural suggestion is that Crayford is Gardiner's nominee on the appraisement, and that Gardiner is the missing fourth owner of the "Mayflower".

Can we make the connection between the two Crayfords and the fourth owner of the "Mayflower" and Gardiner any closer?

For the Crayford clan in Chalfont St. Giles we have a good deal of evidence from the Church Registers, for example :—

> 1586. Richard Craforde, the sonn of Edwarde Craforde, baptised the 25th of September.
>
> 1587. Craforde Cheeke the son of Richard Cheeke was baptised the xxist of December. (Note that his mother was Mistress Margaret Gardiner.)
>
> 1600. An. Craforde the wife of Ric. Craford Esquier, was buried the first day of August.
>
> 1603/4. Mr. Ric. Crayforde, Esquier, was buried the xviiith of January.
>
> 1614/15. William Alder and Jane Craiford married 15 December.
>
> 1620/21 (sic). Mrs. Crayford, widow, buried 21 July.

After which they do not appear again till 1662 when there are many entries for Chalfont and Amersham, with the spelling Crafford.

Here is evidence enough of the connection of Richard Crayford ("cousin Crayford") and the Gardiners ; they disappear from the parish records quite early in the century. It does not really add to what we knew already.

At the Rotherhithe end of the line the clan is still harder to trace. Thomas Crayford of Rotherhithe is described as a mariner, which does not take us far. I have not succeeded in finding him, but there is a *William* Craford, mariner of Ipswich, who is mentioned in one of the *Privy Signet Bills* for the second year of James I. (May, 1605). The document is as follows :—

Warrant to William Craford, John Crane, William Hamon, John Lowe, John Chaplyn, Thomas Cock, William Cock and partners, of Ipswich, mariners, and Edward Howard and partners of "Olborowe," mariners, for tonnage on the "Goodwill," "Isaac," "Diligent," "Swan" and "Vineyard," all of Ipswich, and the "Mary" of Aldeburgh. "One crown of the double rose of the value of five shillings" for every ton, in all 1302 crowns, to be received of William Garroway, Francis Jones and Nicholas Salter, farmers of the customs.

The interest of the document lies in finding a Crayford, a mariner, in the district from which the second "Mayflower" came (and perhaps the first also). It suggests the Crayford people as the reason for building the new ship at Aldeburgh. This is shadowy enough, but it is perhaps in such directions that the final solution may come, and the connection between Crayford the mariner and Gardiner the landowner and shipowner become definitely attested.

The other direction in which to look for the link between Gardiner, the owner of Jordans farm, and the "Mayflower," is through Richard Gardiner who sailed in the "Mayflower," and left the colony to die, apparently at an early date. We have credited this Richard Gardiner with an origin at Coles Hill, between Amersham and the Chalfonts. This brings him very close, indeed, to the Gardiner family of Chalfont St. Giles. But the difficulty that arises is this, that the name *Richard*

Gardiner does not appear in the Inquisitions and Wills that we have been examining. In the adjacent Chesham district, we can find, however, another Gardiner clan, probably related to those who own Jordans farm, and here we come across the missing Richard Gardiner. We can trace this family by their wills in the Archdeaconry of Bucks ; they appear to be freeholders, farming their own estates. In the will of John Gardiner (21 Jan. 1595/6) of White End, Great Chesham, one of the witnesses is Richard Gardiner. This might very well be the "Mayflower" man.

There is another Richard Gardiner, a maltster of Great Chesham, whose will was proved on 28 September, 1591. In the case of the Chesham Parish Registers, we are splendidly provided with material for our quest, in the edition of them furnished by Mr. Garrett-Pegge. Here we find at once a great number of Gardiners, especially those bearing the names of John and Richard. Among the burial records, we have a possible choice between

5 April, 1624.   Richard the son of William Gardiner.

13 July, 1635.   Richard Gardiner.

One of these dates may be that of the lost "Mayflower" Pilgrim. Further investigation may make this clearer. As the case stands, the argument is acquiring unity and approaching completion. We may sum up our investigation in the following manner :—

1. There is some tradition that the old barn at Jordans was built out of the wood of the "Mayflower".

2. Since the "Mayflower" of the Pilgrims was broken up in 1624, the barn should have been built at that time, if the tradition is correct, and if it refers to that particular "Mayflower".

3. It is certain that the barn was built out of the

timbers of a ship of the size of the Pilgrims' "Mayflower," and that it was put together by shipwrights from the Thames.

4. The neighbouring farm-house was rebuilt, in part, out of the same ship's timber, and at a date 1618 or later.

5. The barn has been raised on brick foundations, with bricks of an earlier date than 1625.

6. It has a cracked middle beam as the "Mayflower" had, but this feature may be non-significant.

7. It has been thought to have the name of Harwich, the port of registry of the Pilgrims' "Mayflower," on one of its beams. This feature may be the result of imagination.

8. The farm-house, which, as we said, employed timber from the same ship, has an old door, which is covered with floral emblems, which may stand for "Mayflowers".

9. One of the principal owners of the "Mayflower," Robert Child, lived only a few miles from the Jordans farm, at Amersham or in the neighbourhood. Another of the owners, named Moore, bears a familiar county name.

10. A passenger in the "Mayflower," named Richard Gardiner, may be traced to the same neighbourhood ; he left the colony, returned to England, and appears to have been buried at Chesham.

11. The actual owner of the farm, named Gardiner, was the builder of the ship-barn at Jordans, and was related to the family of one of the persons, named Crayford, who appraised the "Mayflower" when she was broken up. Gardiner is the missing fourth owner of the ship.

12. The appraiser, in question, had a relative at

Ipswich, like himself a shipman, who may have been responsible for the building of the second "Mayflower," at Aldburgh, instead of on the Thames.

The conclusion at which we arrive is, that

THE SHIP OUT OF WHICH THE BARN WAS BUILT

WAS

THE "MAYFLOWER".

CHAPTER XIII

CONCLUDING REMARKS.

IF the arguments of the foregoing pages are valid, and we have substantiated in a satisfactory manner the local tradition relating to the Old Barn at Jordans, then the "Mayflower" is in the possession of the Society of Friends. The first thing that arises in one's mind, in view of such a conclusion is, that in that case we are face to face with one of the ironies of history ; for it cannot be said that the Pilgrims, if they could have willed their property away, would have made such a bequest. Even at New Plymouth, the Quaker invasion of the Pilgrims which occurred nearly forty years after their first arrival, was not received amicably. They did not, indeed, proceed to apply Boston methods to the intruders, and the ancient leaven was still operative when Isaac Robinson, the son of their founder, went into disfranchisement rather than become a persecutor ; but the general criticism was hostile, and there was occasional violence along with the expression of adverse judgment. This is curious, in view of the fact that both the Pilgrims and the Quakers were the victims of the same hostile legislation. And now the Friends have the sacred symbol of liberty, which we know was not a Ship of Fools, a Navis Stultifera, in their own keeping. As we said, that is one of the ironies of history ; well, the ironies of history are the judgments of time, and have a sanctity of their own. A good instance, in our own day, of a similar judgment occurred when the slaves of Jefferson Davis got the ownership of their master's old farm. These things are sometimes called the whirligig of time, as in the Shakespearian phrase, " The whirligig of time brings in its revenges "; but the term is too light and too slight to express the cyclical motion of events ; we ought to find a better symbol than a whirligig, and the revenge, if it is one, is agreeable to both of the parties involved.

> Now God be praised! said Alice the nurse ;
> That all comes round so just and fair.

Then, in the next place, as we have already foreshadowed in our remarks on the possible removal of the bones of Penn, there is no prospect of taking this great relic away from where it stands.   It is as valuable as Stonehenge, and must not be disturbed.   Indeed there is a limit to the extent to which appropriation of British treasures is lawful by our friends on the other side.   If they take all our monuments away, they will presently leave us as barren of historical interest as the Rock of Ormuz, and have no further reason for believing that we are, and must be, one people, bound together by the closest spiritual and historical ties.   The Friends will keep firm hold of their end of the new Anglo-American chain which has come to light.   It is a new cable laid between Plymouth Old and Plymouth New, and the hinterlands of both Plymouths, along which messages of brotherly kindness and charity and heart-felt sympathies, outlasting local and temporary misunderstandings, and "late unpleasantnesses" may pass and repass for ever.

The first actual greeting which the Friends allow to pass is from Old Plymouth; it is a great city now, of nearly a quarter of a million inhabitants. They have a splendid historical record (the "Mayflower" incident being one of the stars in their firmament), but alas! they are almost entirely destitute of the higher learning and the facilities for it. They want to place an Anglo-American and International College on the heights above the town, which history has made famous. Come over into Macedonia and help us—to help ourselves to such a splendid consummation. Do for us what you have done for Constantinople. Half of its halls shall bear the names of Washington and Lincoln, and we can find as good a site for a statue of Liberty enlightening the world as even the harbour of New York itself.

Made in the USA
Monee, IL
15 September 2022

14089942R00059